JUUL FINED $438.5 MILLION: How They Got Here, The Rise, Products, Ban , Lawsuits And Settlement

Wilhelm Coast

TABLE OF CONTENT

CHAPTER ONE

THE JUUL LABS

In 2017, JUUL, a well-known American e-cigarette manufacturer, separated from Pax Labs. The Juul electronic cigarette, created by Juul Labs, atomizes nicotine salts made from tobacco that are delivered via single-use, non-refillable cartridges they call JUULpods. The contents within the pod are heated by the e-cigarette device's battery to produce vapor that the user inhales. A pack of cigarettes would approximately be the comparison for each pod.

On May 22, 2015, James Monsees and Adam Bowen co-founded Juul Labs, which has its headquarters in San Francisco. On December 20, 2018, Altria (formerly Philip Morris Companies) paid $12.8 billion for a 35% share in Juul Labs. A $2 billion incentive was given to Juul, which would be shared among its 1,500 staff members.

After a significant social media effort, Juul became the most well-liked e-cigarette in the US by the end of 2017, and as of September 2018, it had a 72% market share.

Given the high nicotine concentrations in Juul, the potential health effects of its use by young people could be more severe than those from their use of other e-cigarette products, which has raised concerns from the public health community and prompted numerous investigations by the U.S. Food and Drug Administration (FDA). According to an FDA probe in 2018, Juul agreed to remove from the market several flavored cartridges that would tempt minors to use them. The corporation and the Center for Environmental Health achieved a settlement in 2019 wherein the company agreed to reduce and confine its marketing efforts to people who are of the proper age.

On June 23, 2022, the FDA rejected Juul's request for permission to keep selling its products in the country and issued Marketing Denial Orders (MDOs) that immediately forbade any further promotion or sale of the goods.

The next day, the U.S. Court of Appeals in Washington, D.C., blocked that order.

HOW JUUL IS BORN

Before developing Juul, Adam Bowen and James Monsees, who had met while taking product design classes at Stanford University in 2015, developed an e-cigarette called Ploom and the Pax vaporizer for cannabis and loose-leaf tobacco.

In 2007, they launched a company with the same name. The business created Juul in 2015, sold Ploom and changed its name to Pax Labs. On May 22, 2015, Juul Labs, Inc. was established. Pax Labs unveiled the Juul electronic cigarette in June 2015.

Tyler Goldman, the former CEO of PAX Labs, was selected as the CEO of Juul after the firm was split out from PAX Labs in July 2017. Goldman was replaced by Kevin Burns in December 2017 James Monsees, a co-founder, served as Juul's Chief Product Officer and board member. Co-founder Adam Bowen served as a director and Juul's chief technology officer. Nicholas Pritzker, whose family controlled the large chewing tobacco company Conwood, Riaz Valani, and Hoyoung Huh are other board members.

By the end of 2018, 1,500 workers were working with the firm, up from 200 in September 2017.

The Juul e-cigarette is now built in Shenzhen, China, while the pods are produced in the United States as of July 2018. Another name for pods is "vape juice."

One of the biggest cigarette producers in the world, Altria, paid $12.8 billion for 35% of Juul on December 20, 2018. In 2019, Juul invested over $400 million in a San Francisco skyscraper.

Martha Coakley, a former attorney general of Massachusetts, joined Juul in April 2018. She works on the government relations team to organize lobbying for the product while promoting use restrictions for minors.

The United States House of Representatives opened an inquiry into Juul Labs on June 13, 2019, focusing on the company's commercial partnership with Altria, social media and advertising strategies, and communications. Raja Krishnamoorthi, a representative from Illinois and the leader of the oversight committee for economic and consumer policy, led the inquiry. Juul "appears to be breaching FDA restrictions barring making unapproved direct and implied claims that its product helps consumers quit smoking cigarettes and is safer than cigarettes," according to the panel.

On September 25, 2019, it was revealed that Kevin Burns will step down as CEO and be replaced by K.C. Crosthwaite, Altria's chief growth officer.

Several leaders left the firm in October 2019, including Senior Vice President of advanced technologies David Foster, Chief Administrative Officer Ashley Gould, Chief Marketing Officer Craig Brommers, and Chief Financial Officer Tim Danaher.

On October 31, 2019, Altria said that $4.5 billion of its investment in Juul will be written down. In October 2020, Altria valued Juul at around $10 billion. By March 2021, that value had dropped to $4.3 billion, and by March 2022, it had fallen to $1.6 billion.

EXECUTIVE GROUP

Since 2019, K. C. Crosthwaite has served as the CEO of Juul. James Monsees is the founder and chief product officer, while Adam Bowen is the chief technology officer. [45] Juul's chief regulatory officer is Jose Luis Murillo. He formerly served as Altria's Senior Vice President of Regulatory Affairs.

CHAPTER TWO

WHAT IS JUUL?

JUUL is a vaporizer, commonly referred to as an electronic cigarette or e-cigarette, that is unique from all others and was created with adult smokers in mind. Innovative vapor technology has never been more pleasurable thanks to our unique, nicotine-containing e-liquid composition.

JUUL DEVICE

The Juul device is a closed system vaporizer designed for adult smokers who want to quit cigarettes. It offers a straightforward and consistently gratifying experience.

The JUUL Device consists of:

- charging connections on the bottom that link your device to the USB Charging Dock.
- an indicator light that indicates charge.
- an aperture where you insert the JUULpod.

The JUUL Device has a stress-tested battery, a temperature control system, and sensors that detect when it is being used.

THE JULLPOD

An exclusive nicotine-containing e-liquid composition is contained in a disposable, non-refillable cartridge known as a JUULpod, which offers a pleasurable experience. There is no need to use up your JUULpod before replacing it since they are not refillable. You just need to choose the flavor and level of nicotine, and you're ready to begin.

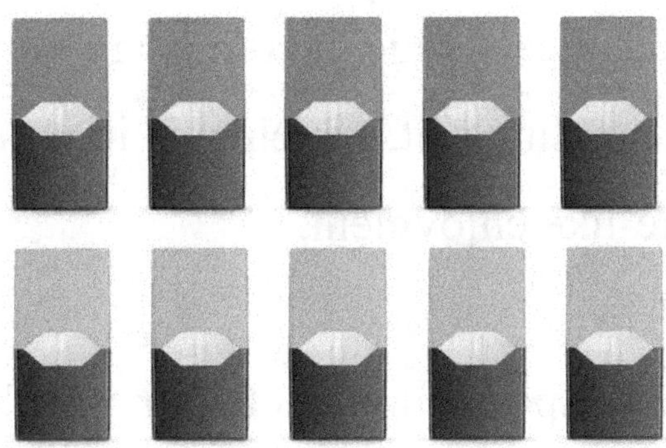

HOW JUULPOD FUNCTIONS?

As a mouthpiece, the JUULpod snaps into the top of the JUUL Device. New hardware is included with each JUULpod, so there are no components to change and no setup steps. Propylene glycol and glycerol of pharmaceutical grade are used to make Juul pod. which, when heated, produces an aerosol that contains flavors, benzoic acid, and nicotine. Benzoic acid and pharmaceutical-grade nicotine are mixed to form a nicotine salt, which aids in producing cigarette-like enjoyment.

Each JUULpod's unique flavor profile may be achieved by combining natural and artificial elements in the flavoring.

THE DESIGN

The Juul e-cigarette is recharged using a magnetic USB dock and resembles a USB flash drive in appearance.

In contrast to the majority of earlier generations of e-cigarettes, which utilized free-base nicotine, Juul e-cigarettes employ nicotine salts (protonated nicotine). The major source of nicotine is tobacco.

Juul aims to give a nicotine peak in five minutes, comparable to a regular cigarette, therefore the nicotine salts are supposed to produce an experience more akin to smoking than other e-cigarettes on the market.

In contrast to tobacco smoke, the nicotine salts soften the harshness of the Juul aerosol. Because it seems to enable users to inhale far larger nicotine doses than they would otherwise be able to, the protonated nicotine formulation of nicotine salts has been characterized as problematic. An average of 200 puffs are produced by each cartridge, also known as a "JUULpod" or "JUUL pod," which has roughly the same amount of nicotine as a pack of cigarettes. Each cartridge contains far more nicotine than the majority of e-cigarettes currently on the market (59 mg/ml in the US, 20 mg/ml in the EU). Juul debuted 3 percent-strength pods in August 2018 for its mint and Virginia tobacco tastes. This translates to 30 mg/ml. Propylene glycol, glycerin, flavorings, and nicotine salts are all included in each cartridge. Up to the end of 2019, Juul pods were available in eight flavors, with mango being the most popular.

TASTE POD

The flavors of Juul Labs' JUULpods include:

- **Virginia Tobacco:** The flavor of the flue-cured Virginia tobacco is distinctive. JUULpods made with Virginia tobacco have a robust taste with earthy undertones and a smooth finish.

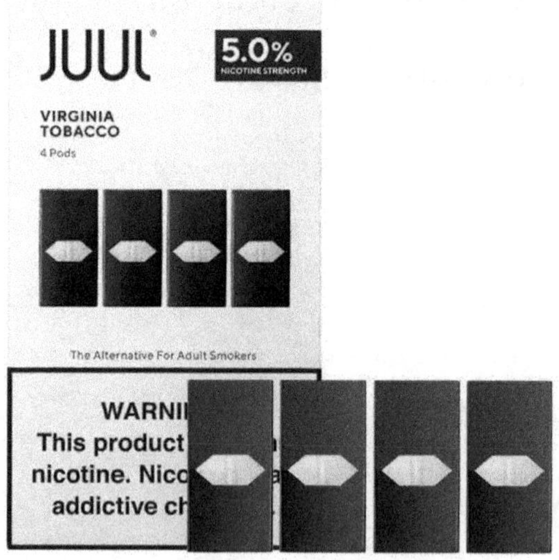

- **Menthol JUULpods:** They provide a very crisp classic taste because of the time and work JUUL Labs has put into making them. You'll get a surge of menthol while using Menthol JUULpods, followed by a sharp aftertaste.

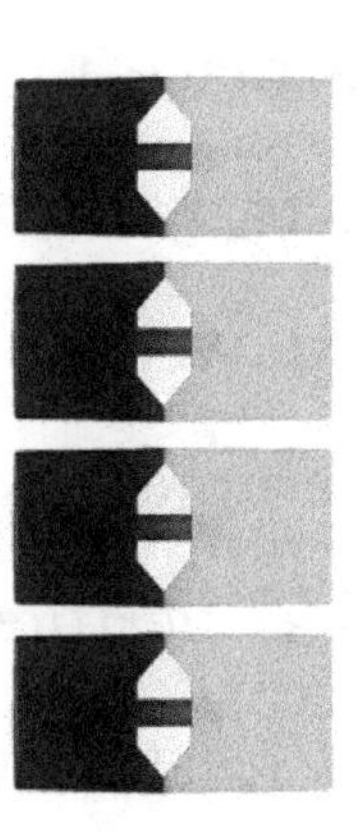

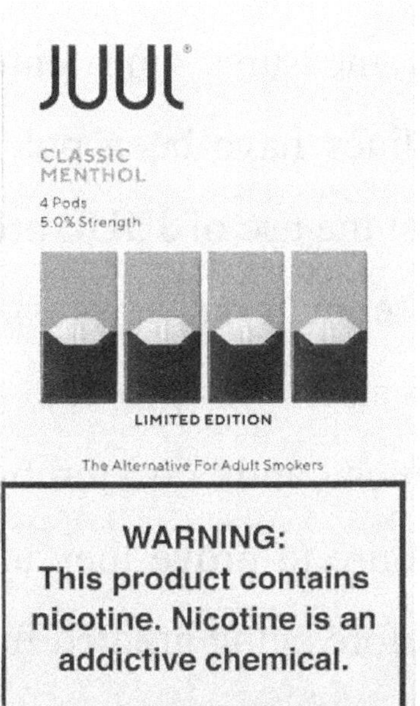

CHAPTER THREE

JUUL USAGE

JUUL was designed exclusively for adult smokers. Juul was developed primarily for adult smokers since ending the use of combustible cigarettes requires that those who have never used nicotine never start. Extra measures and cutting-edge security guidelines have been put into place to fight against the use of JUUL products by minors.

JUUL.com is an age-restricted website that needs users to provide government-issued identities and go through a verification procedure to prove they are at least 21 years old before being granted full access.

However the use of Juul is being found to be common among adolescents (teenagers).

JUUL AND ADOLESCENT

Teenagers have grown to love Juul's products, which has the public health profession worried that long-term trends in juvenile nicotine use are being reversed. According to a study conducted on 13,000 Americans in October 2018, 9.5% of teenagers between the ages of 15 and 17 and 11% of young adults between the ages of 18 and 21 currently use Juul. Teenagers between the ages of 15 and 17 are 16 times more likely to use Juul than people between the ages of 25 and 34. One in five students between the ages of 12 and 17 had seen a Juul being used in a school setting, which shows how prevalent Juul usage is among middle-level and high school students. When using Juul, teenagers refer to it as "Juuling."

According to the 2018 National Drug Trends, teens are using e-cigarettes like Juul more often. As they have over the last 20 years, cigarette smoking rates among 12th grade students have decreased. On the other side, the rise in vaping rates from 2017 to 2018 was the biggest disparity seen since the 1975 start of the survey. Researchers speculate that this may be because there are many educational initiatives in place to inform young people of the dangers of cigarette smoking, while there are currently few initiatives for vaping products. From 11% in 2017 to 21% in 2018, the proportion of students in the 12th grade who reported vaping nicotine nearly doubled. In the 10th grade, the proportion increased from 8% to 16%. In addition, a Truth Initiative survey revealed that 56% of teenagers who use Juul do so more than three times each month. The Juul was reportedly used more than 10 times per month by over 25% of youngsters. These results imply that teens are regularly using Juuls rather than merely dabbling with them. This seems to be at odds with the assertion made by Juul's developers, James Monsees and Adam Bowen, that the device's goal is to enhance adult smokers' lives by doing away with cigarettes.

Juul's appeal among teens has been attributed to a variety of factors, including young people's false belief that it is safe, its simplicity to hide, its slick, high-tech appearance, and its fruity pod tastes. Direct marketing to teenagers may have also been a factor. The Massachusetts Attorney General's office revealed in February 2020 that evidence it had gathered during its investigation showed that the business had purchased advertising space on websites for middle school students' homework, such as CoolMathGames.com, Seventeen magazine, Nickolodeon, and Nick Jr.

63% of teenagers and young adults did not know that the Juul products they used always included nicotine, according to the 2017 Truth Initiative poll. Because many of the hazards associated with e-cigarettes and Juul usage are still unclear, there aren't many educational programs or public health campaigns on these products.

Juul is discretely used even in class because of its size, shape, and similarity to a flash drive. Its low vapor production and delicate aroma, which may be mistaken for perfume, also make it easier to hide. As a result, it is simple to hide in clothes or other places. For example, a high school in Newton, Massachusetts found a Juul disguised as a Sharpie. Juul's tiny and high-tech form, which is evocative of the iPhone, as well as its appeal among young people, are additional often mentioned factors.

Teenagers are particularly drawn to Juul's sweet tastes, notably the fruit and crème brûlée ones. Juuls may produce a fruity fragrance when vaped, in contrast to the smell of cigarette smoke. In a 2016 CDC and FDA research, 31% of middle and high school adolescents who use e-cigarettes said they did so because flavors were readily available. Juul said it "heard the concerns" and "responded by simplifying the names and deleting the adjectives" after renaming various tastes, including "cold cucumber" to "cucumber", "creme brûlée" to "creme", and "classic menthol" to "menthol". To stop the rise in adolescent consumption, Juul stopped producing all flavored pods in November 2018.

Young people were the focus of several of Juul's early marketing efforts, which made heavy use of social media, had kid-friendly themes, and featured young models holding Juuls. Juul spent thousands of dollars in July 2019 promoting Juul as a smoking cessation tool to children in schools. Juul misrepresented itself as being "totally safe" and offered young people the chance to work as brand ambassadors. In reaction to the FDA crackdown on Juul, the business said that genuine consumers who were using the device to quit smoking will be used instead of models. Juul has stopped using social media as of November 2018.

According to a Truth Initiative poll conducted in May 2018, 74% of Juul users between the ages of 12 and 17 got their device via a physical retailer, 52% from a friend or relative, and 6% through the internet (respondents could select multiple answers). Juul believes that 90% of its sales take place in physical locations. According to the poll, 89% of young people's efforts to purchase Juuls online were successful. Juul updated its age verification procedures in October 2018 in response to FDA criticism, requiring personnel to manually compare drivers' licenses to public databases for precise matches. As a result, anybody under the age of 21 was rejected, but many adults were also rejected or discouraged.

HEALTH ISSUES

It is uncertain how vaping affects Juul users, particularly children. Longitudinal clinical trials have not been performed as of yet. 2019 research indicated that Juul pods were the only product to show in vitro cytotoxicity from both nicotine and taste chemical content, particularly ethyl maltol. This research sampled a variety of e-cigarette delivery devices. Vape liquid pods are noted for their unpredictable nicotine delivery that often deviates from the labeling and may include a wide range of other substances. Propylene glycol, which has been shown to cause deep airway inflammation and airway epithelial damage, is also included in these liquid pods. Following a report on vaping-related lung illness in the US, a large number of individuals started tweeting about quitting their Juuls within the next 24 hours.

JUULS' NICOTINE CONTENT

The nicotine content of one Juul pod is equivalent to that of one to two packs of cigarettes. Juuls have a greater nicotine level than other e-cigarette brands; their volume of e-liquid contains 5% nicotine, which is almost twice as much as other brands. Additionally, Juul pods include much more benzoic acid per milliliter (44.8 mg/mL) than other brands, which have between 0.2 and 2 mg/mL. Benzoic acid exposure regularly might cause stomach aches, a sore throat, and coughing. Robert Jackler, director of Stanford Research into the Impact of Tobacco Advertising, said in 2019: "When Juul came out with extremely high-nicotine electronic cigarettes, it prompted a nicotine arms race by competitor firms wanting to mimic the success of Juul." The highest legal limit for the amount of nicotine permitted in its pods is 1.7% in certain areas, including Israel, although Juul does not sell this level in the US. Low-dose or zero-dose nicotine pods are not available from Juul.

Juuls differ from other e-cigarettes in that they mimic the effects of traditional cigarettes by using nicotine salts rather than freebase nicotine. Inhaling nicotine salts is made simpler by the fact that they are less acidic than freebase nicotine. Additionally, nicotine salts are more quickly and at a comparable rate to regular cigarettes absorbed into circulation. Users may not be aware of how much nicotine they are consuming since it doesn't irritate them and is easy to inhale. Given Juul's high nicotine content, its usage by young people may have greater detrimental effects on their health than their use of other e-cigarette products.

TYPICAL ADVERSE EFFECTS

On the body and the psyche, nicotine has a variety of impacts, including:

a diminished appetite

- Diarrhea
- Intestinal Discomfort
- Enhanced Mood Better Concentration And Memory
- Higher Blood Pressure
- Higher Heart Rate
- Increased Phlegm And Saliva Production
- Nausea
- Sweating

"We don't worry a lot about addiction here because we're not trying to create a cessation product at all," R&D engineer Ari Atkins of Pax Labs said.

"Anything regarding health is not on our thoughts," he said. FDA Commissioner Dr. Scott Gottlieb said that the nicotine in Juul is enough to cause addiction in April 2018. "In some situations, our youngsters are trying these products and enjoying them without even realizing they include nicotine," said Gottlieb. And that's a concern because, as we all know, nicotine in these items may change how teenage brains develop, creating years of addiction. [112]

News reports from the end of 2018 mentioned rising Juul addiction rates among teenagers, which harm relationships and brain development.

Due to nicotine's addictive qualities, Juul's high nicotine level has raised concerns. The FDA has set a public hearing on juvenile vaping cessation for January 18, 2019, in response to concerns that have been raised over the lack of therapies for teenage vaping cessation.

CHAPTER FOUR

HISTORY OF E-CIGARETTE REGULATIONS BY THE FDA

In 2007, when the first electronic cigarettes were sold, the FDA lacked the power to control them. The FDA didn't get the ability to regulate e-cigarettes until 2016. Juul had already taken over as the leading brand at that point.

The National Institutes of Health revealed in research that record percentages of American teenagers were vaping on December 17, 2018. Just one day later, to save the nation's kids from what he termed an "epidemic" of e-cigarette usage, the U.S. Surgeon General urged that local governments outlaw indoor vaping and impose taxes on e-cigarette sales.

TIMELINE FOR JUUL AND E-CIGARETTE REGULATION

2007	The United States saw the introduction of e-cigarettes
2015	Juul introduces itself
2016	The FDA was initially granted the power to control e-cigarettes.

2017	The FDA unveiled its Comprehensive Plan for Nicotine and Tobacco Regulation.
April 2018	Juul was asked for information by the FDA on its marketing and studies about juvenile start and usage, and more than 1,300 warning letters and penalties were issued to merchants that unlawfully supplied Juul and other e-cigarettes to minors.

July 2019	Reporting of the first instances of EVALI (e-cigarette or vaping device use-related lung damage)
2019 September	Juul received a warning letter from the FDA for advertising its products as "safer than tobacco" to young people, and the FDA has started

	completing the premarket authorization criteria for e-cigarettes without tobacco flavors.
September 2019	The first e-cigarette to submit Premarket Tobacco Product Applications (PMTAs) to the FDA is Reynolds American's Vuse. Juul stopped selling vape pods with fruit and dessert flavors.
2019 September	Deadline for submitting PMTAs for all e-cigarettes to

	keep promoting and selling in the United States.
Nov. 20, 2021	FDA published final guidelines for premarket applications for tobacco products (PMTAs)
June 2022	Due to a lack of information in its PMTA, the FDA issued marketing denial orders (MDOs) for all Juul products, prohibiting their sale and distribution in the United States.

July 2022	FDA placed a moratorium on Juul MDOs.

Patient advocacy and medical organizations, including the American Medical Association, supported the FDA's ban on Juul devices. The majority of people are optimistic that Juul goods won't be sold.

"According to AMA policy, all e-cigarette and vaping products should be banned from sale and distribution, except for those that have been FDA-approved for use in helping people quit smoking. The American Medical Association (AMA) has advocated for stricter regulations to shield young people from the negative consequences of tobacco and nicotine use and will continue to do so since identifying e-cigarette usage and vaping as an urgent public health pandemic in 2018.

HOW DOES THE FDA EXAMINE JUUL AND OTHER ELECTRONIC CIGARETTE BUSINESSES?

The FDA examines data and information businesses provide in a **Premarket Tobacco Product Application** (PMTA) while reviewing Juul and other e-cigarettes . A PMTA "must offer scientific evidence that proves a product is suitable for the protection of public health," according to the FDA. In 2021, the agency published its codified recommendations for PMTA content and structure.

PMTAs include information on the product's health hazards and if those risks are more or fewer than those of other tobacco products already on the market. It must also provide facts on the product's manufacturing process, ingredients, additives, and how the e-cigarette device functions. Among other criteria, manufacturers must provide samples of the product and a suggested label.

To discuss the PMTA procedure, the FDA meets with the producer. The agency then confirms that the application satisfies the requirements for evaluation. The FDA starts its real assessment of the data and information given if it satisfies the requirements. The FDA will determine whether to issue a marketing permitted order or a marketing denial order based on this.

CHAPTER FIVE

JUUL LAWSUITS' CURRENT STATE

3,986 Juul cases from all across the country were consolidated in multidistrict litigation (MDL), MDL-2913, as of July 15, 2022.
Juul disputes claims made in many cases that its advertising is directed at adolescents.

Juul Labs claimed they have never advertised to minors and do not wish any non-nicotine consumers to test our products. "These cases mostly repeat false claims that have already been made in other litigation, which we have been vigorously battling for more than a year. We shall continue to uphold our purpose notwithstanding the lack of validity in these instances.

Both class action lawsuits and individual personal injury complaints filed in four states were included in the cases. It is anticipated that the dispute will only intensify.

In addition, Juul Labs Inc. has been sued by a number of states for its role in the adolescent vaping pandemic. Juul agreed to pay North Carolina $40 million as part of the first state litigation settlement in June 2021. At least nine other states have filed legal action.

JUUL E-CIGARETTE LAWSUIT CLAIMS

Juul advertised its goods in a way that would appeal to young people.

The nicotine products are more strong and addicting than tobacco cigarettes wasn't disclosed in its marketing.

The company's goods are flawed and excessively risky.
The mass litigation has no currently planned trials.

Before news of widespread lung ailments and fatalities linked to vaping started to surface in the middle of 2019, the majority of the early cases in the mass litigation were submitted. According to a New York Times article from October 2019, some of the sickened individuals had previously consumed nicotine products under the Juul brand.

JUUL IS BEING SUED FOR WRONGFUL DEATH

In October 2019, the first wrongful death case against Juul was filed in a federal court in California.

David Wakefield, 18, allegedly started vaping after being exposed to Juul marketing when he was 15 and kept doing so for years, according to his mother.

According to the lawsuit, Wakefield had respiratory and lung issues that necessitated a three-day hospital stay a year after he began vaping. The medical personnel had to apply nicotine patches on him to curb his urges since he was so hooked to nicotine.

Wakefield carried on vaping after leaving the hospital. The lawsuit states that the father discovered the youngster had passed away in his sleep early on August 31, 2019.

According to the complaint, Juul sold its products to minors and that Wakefield's death was significantly influenced by the company's "actions and the faults in Juul products."

CASES IN COURT ONE MILLION TAINTED VAPE PODS WERE SOLD BY JUUL.

In October 2019, a former senior vice president of Juul sued the firm, saying he was let go after raising concerns over 1 million tainted, mint-flavored Juul pods that were sent to merchants and customers. The precise kind of contamination was not identified in the case.

Juul "refused to recall those tainted pods or even provide a product health and safety warning," according to Siddharth Breja's complaint. Additionally, despite his repeated complaints, the firm was accused of selling outdated goods.

Kevin Burns, the organization's former CEO, said on CBS This Morning in September 2019 that Juul's products were assessed for toxicity and legality. He said that Juul wouldn't market a hazardous product.

The complaint makes no mention of the contaminated pods or the 2019 EVALI (e-cigarette, or vaping, product use related lung injury) epidemic. Additionally, it makes no reference to any additional harms associated with vaping.

VAPING IS BLAMED IN LAWSUITS FOR BREATHING ISSUES

People who were hospitalized or who lost loved ones to EVALI (**e-cigarette or vaping use-associated lung injury**) are likely to file lawsuits. The lung harm caused by vaping was first noted in the middle of 2019, and it soon affected hundreds of individuals.

The American Centers for Disease Control and Prevention have recorded 2,807 hospitalized instances of the lung damage as of February 18, 2020. At same time, the CDC also reported 68 EVALI-related fatalities.

The CDC had concluded that vitamin E acetate was "strongly connected to the EVALI epidemic" by early 2020. The material is used to thicken vape fluids, especially those that contain THC, the main psychoactive component of marijuana.

The FDA issued marketing denial orders (MDOs) in June 2022, resulting in a Juul ban that forbade the sale of vaping goods in the United States. The FDA did, however, suspend the restriction in July 2022 while it looked at further information. Juul products continue to be available in the United States up until further notice.

Similar vaping prohibitions have been implemented in San Francisco and other cities and states.

LUNG INJURY AND JUUL LUNG DISEASE LAWSUITS

According to complaints filed by other e-cigarette users, toxins in e-cigarette fluids contributed to bronchiolitis obliterans organizing pneumonia, or BOOP. In still other claims, it is alleged that vaping contributed to hemorrhagic strokes, which happen when bleeding abruptly affects the brain.

A lawsuit was launched in 2019 by two Alabama college students who said that using Juul e-cigarettes caused major lung diseases. Elizabeth Swearingen attended the University of Alabama when she was 19 years old. She had participated in cross country in high school. She "now has problems breathing throughout the simplest of duties," the complaint states,

A 19-year-old Auburn University student named John Thomas Via Peavy has been smoking Juul e-cigarettes since he was 17 years old. He allegedly had "serious respiratory issues after taking Juul," according to the complaint. According to the complaint, Peavy's chest congestion and appetite loss have not improved.

According to the lawsuit, Swearingen and Peavy both inadvertently ingested vape liquids while using Juuls.

According to a 2018 research published in the journal Thorax, e-cigarette vapor impairs lung immune cells and worsens inflammation. According to research, it may raise the risk of COPD, or chronic obstructive lung disease.

The symptoms of COPD are comparable to those of bronchiolitis obliterans organizing pneumonia, or BOOP, another lung ailment. The American Lung Association has issued a warning that BOOP is a possible adverse effect of vaping.

CASES IN COURT JUUL PODS' NICOTINE CONTENT CAUSED SEIZURES

The American Food and Drug Administration started looking into allegations of seizures linked to vaping in April 2019. Teenagers and young adults were the main subjects of the reports. While the FDA inquiry was still ongoing, a few individuals who had these seizures started bringing legal claims.

After the 15-year-old Florida girl began experiencing seizures, her parents sued Juul Labs, Altria Group Inc., and Philip Morris USA Inc. in 2019. They claimed that the teenager's seizures were caused by nicotine poisoning from vaping. According to Erin and Jared NesSmith, their daughter developed a Juul e-cigarette addiction. Each Juul vape pod has the same amount of nicotine as a pack of traditional cigarettes.

She allegedly ingested e-cig liquids while using a Juul, according to the complaint.

The FDA has recorded 127 complaints of seizures or other neurological symptoms that occurred between 2010 and 2019 as of the month of August. Many of these situations might lead to e-cigarette lawsuits.

The harmful effects of nicotine include seizures. But many teenagers are unaware of the dangers of nicotine in e-cigarettes. According to a 2019 research published in the journal Pediatrics, 40% of teenagers were unaware that the vape fluids they were using included nicotine.

The FDA discovered that teenagers and young adults were involved in many of the seizure complaints it looked at. North

Carolina resident Luka Kinard had convulsions after vaping the equivalent of 80 tobacco cigarettes daily. According to a story in the Greensboro News & Record, the boy, who was 14 at the time, had to enter treatment to kick his nicotine habit.

SUIT ALLEGES MAN'S JUUL USE LED TO A MAJOR STROKE

Maxwell Berger filed a lawsuit against Juul Labs in 2019 alleging that his two Juul pod habit per day caused his severe stroke before he turned 20. He would have consumed the same amount of nicotine by vaping two of the pods as he would by smoking 40 cigarettes of traditional tobacco each day.

In his case, Berger said that in 2015, while he was still a senior in high school, he began smoking a Juul e-cigarette. Two years later, he allegedly used the gadget every ten minutes due to his extreme nicotine addiction.

In July 2017, he had a sizable hemorrhagic stroke. When a blood artery ruptures close to the brain, hemorrhagic strokes may result. Blood accumulates within the skull, placing pressure on the brain and causing damage.

According to Berger's complaint, he had three brain operations and needed to stay in the hospital for 100 days as a consequence. According to the complaint, the man has left-side paralysis, communication problems, and visual loss in both eyes of 50%.

A 2019 research revealed that e-cigarette users have greater risks of stroke and cardiac issues than non-users at the International Stroke Conference. Researchers discovered that e-cigarette users had a 71 percent greater risk of stroke, a 59 percent higher risk of heart attack, and a 40 percent higher risk of heart disease.

CHAPTER SIX

JUUL'S BAN

The U.S. Food and Drug Administration prohibited the sale and distribution of any Juul products in the country beginning in June 2022. A few days later, the FDA put the prohibition on hold while they conducted further research. Before this, governments and municipalities tried to outlaw or limit Juul on their own due to addiction and lung damage.

JUUL PROHIBITED IN AMERICA

On June 23, 2022, the U.S. Food and Drug Administration (FDA) issued marketing denial orders (MDOs) prohibiting Juul products from being marketed in the country; however, the FDA has since restricted administrative hold until it can reevaluate Juul's marketing application.

The marketing denial order was administratively delayed by the FDA on July 5, 2022. The organization has decided that certain scientific problems with the JUUL application call for further investigation. The FDA noted in its statement that the administrative stay "temporarily suspends the marketing denial order pending the further review, but does not revoke it.

Although the FDA has not overturned the restriction, Juul is still permitted to sell its products, including unflavored vape pods, while it is conducting its study. This implies that until the FDA reaches a final determination, individuals may continue to buy Juul products.

WHY DID THE FDA TRY TO OUTLAW JUUL?

Because Juul failed to give sufficient proof that its products were "appropriate for the protection of public health," the FDA attempted to outlaw the firm. Juul, according to the organization, supplied "insufficient and inconsistent" data, making it difficult for the FDA to evaluate Juul's possible negative effects of vaping.

According to experts, the FDA's ban on Juul is a part of a more aggressive campaign against tobacco and nicotine products to lower cancer fatalities in the United States. As part of President Biden's Cancer

Moonshot campaign, banning Juul coupled with cutting the nicotine content in regular cigarettes and prohibiting menthol-flavored products might help save more lives.

AMERICAN CITIES AND STATES AND BANNED JUUL?

Several states and towns have been attempting to outlaw or regulate Juul and other e-cigarettes for years before the FDA's proposed nationwide ban. For instance, North Carolina was the first state to file a lawsuit against Juul for allegedly marketing to teenagers and fueling the pandemic of youth smoking. Juul consented to provide the government with $40 million in 2021.

The American Nonsmokers' Rights Foundation reports that as of July 1, 2022, 25 states will have legislation in place that prohibit the use of e-cigarettes in completely smoke-free places. States have sought to outlaw all e-cigarettes throughout the years, but the majority of these restrictions only apply to flavored goods and online sales.

Federal legislation passed in December 2019 increased the legal age to buy e-cigarettes from 18 to 21. State governments, however, are free to impose their age restrictions.

According to the Public Law Health Center, buyers of vaping items must generally be above the age of 21.

WHICH STATES HAVE ATTEMPTS TO PROHIBIT JUULS AND OTHER ELECTRONIC CIGARETTES?

Cities, counties, and state governments frequently have more flexibility than federal regulators. However, the majority of state efforts to outlaw Juul and other e-cigarette products have run into legal obstacles.

The majority of states with vaping prohibitions in place or planned have just little success. Local vape stores and a vaping trade association, the Vapor Technology Association, have successfully contested some of the state restrictions in court.

Several states have attempted to outlaw Juul and other e-cigarettes, including:

On September 24, 2019, Massachusetts issued a temporary ban on the sale of Juul products as well as all other e-cigarette and vaping goods. Sales made both online and in physical stores were suspended by the order. It finished on December 11, 2019.

On September 18, 2019, Michigan declared a six-month emergency ban on the sale of flavored vaping goods. Businesses that sell vape products tried to halt the ban, but a court sided with the governor and allowed it to go into force on October 1. However, by mid-October, the ban had been overturned.

On September 17, 2019, New York issued a ban on the majority of flavored vaping goods. The menthol-flavored vape items were excluded from the emergency ban, but the restriction was overturned by a state appeals court the night before it was set to take effect.

A measure to ban all flavored vape products in the state was submitted by Ohio State Representative Tom Patton in the Ohio House of Representatives in September 2019, but it hasn't been passed as of yet.

2020 will see the implementation of Gina Raimondo's ban on all vape flavors other than tobacco.

The Washington State Department of Health was ordered to stop implementing an emergency regulation barring flavored vape goods on October 9, 2019, but The Vapor Technology Association and nearby vape businesses filed a lawsuit on October 21 to stop the order.

The Oregon Court of Appeals partly overturned the governor's prohibition on flavored nicotine and cannabis e-cigarette products, which was set to begin on October 19, 2019, for six months. The court judgment would enable nicotine vape goods to continue to be sold at vape shops, but it would keep the prohibition on marijuana vape products in place.

Montana had a 120-day ban that was set to go into effect on October 22, 2019, but just four days before that date, a state court granted a temporary restraining order delaying its execution. The Vapor Technology Association and three vape shops had contended that the prohibition was excessively onerous.

In October 2019, Utah placed temporary restrictions on the sale of flavored nicotine products. According to the law, only specialized tobacco stores in Utah that are overseen and controlled by local health departments are allowed to sell flavored tobacco and vape goods.

While states have mainly failed to outright prohibit e-cigarettes, several have approved legislation that limits their use and sales. According to the CDC, all 50 states and U.S. territories will have laws prohibiting sales to minors by June 30, 2022, except American Samoa and the Marshall Islands.

A retail license is required in 33 jurisdictions for the over-the-counter sale of e-cigarettes, and 17 states have approved indoor air smoke-free legislation outlawing the use of e-cigarettes in bars, restaurants, and private workplaces.

IN WHICH CITIES ARE JUUL AND OTHER VAPING PRODUCTS PROHIBITED?

According to the Campaign for Tobacco-Free Kids, more than 250 cities have either outlawed or limited the sale of flavored tobacco products. Although e-cigarettes are not subject to all municipal regulations, vaping fluids are legally classified as tobacco goods.

Juul and comparable e-cigarettes have been outlawed in the following cities and counties:

In June 2019, San Francisco became the first major American city to outlaw the sale of all e-cigarettes, not just flavored vape juice. Juul invested millions to overturn the law. By a 4-to-1 margin, voters in November 2019 rejected repealing the restriction. A ban on the sale and production of vaping products has been approved to go into force in the city in January 2020.

On October 1, 2019, Los Angeles County outlawed all flavored tobacco products. All flavored vaping products as well as menthol cigarettes and chewing tobacco were subject to prohibition. A ban on flavored cigars, menthol cigarettes, and flavored e-cigarettes was approved by the city council and will take effect in January 2023.

By a 3-2 vote in October 2019, the San Diego County Board of Supervisors decided to ban the sale of any vaping goods, including Juul products, in unincorporated areas for a full year. The board also decided to outlaw flavored nicotine products permanently. The city of San Diego was unaffected by the restriction. Just one month earlier, the city of El Cajon announced that it could be the first in San Diego County to outlaw the sale of vaping items.

California has some of the most comprehensive municipal restrictions on Juul and other vaping devices. According to the Campaign for Tobacco-Free Kids, more than 55 jurisdictions in the state either have legislation restricting the sale of flavored tobacco products, including vape fluids or are exploring prohibitions.

JUUL AND VAPING BANS IN COLLEGES AND HIGH SCHOOLS

The American Nonsmokers' Rights Foundation estimates that as of July 1, 2022, at least 2,253 tribal schools and universities have banned Juul and other vaping devices from being used on their premises. E-cigarettes are not permitted on the grounds of public schools in Arkansas, Washington, or New Hampshire. Additionally, Virginia mandated that local school boards establish vaping prohibitions for each of their respective school districts.

In an attempt to stop children from vaping, several states have increased the minimum age to purchase e-cigarettes and vape items. According to the Public Health Law Center, 43 states will require consumers to be at least 21 to purchase e-cigarettes by June 15, 2022.

According to the National School Boards Association, the majority of school districts have policies in place that classify vaping goods as illegal and prohibit vaping under student behavior codes.

Similar to how municipalities must go through lengthier voting procedures and get public input on any law, university boards may decide to prohibit or limit the use of e-cigarettes more readily than those in towns.

CHAPTER SEVEN

JUUL'S SETTLEMENT

Juul Labs, will shell up roughly $440 million to resolve a two-year probe by 33 states into the marketing of its high-nicotine vaping devices, which have long been held accountable for a spike in adolescent vaping throughout the country.

On behalf of the states and Puerto Rico which banded together in 2020 to investigate Juul's early advertising and claims about the safety and advantages of its technology as a smoking replacement, Connecticut Attorney General William Tong announced the agreement on Tuesday, September 6, 2022.

The agreement ends one of the company's major legal challenges; it still faces nine other cases from other states. Juul is also facing hundreds of individual lawsuits launched on behalf of young people and others who claim they developed vaping addictions after using the company's devices.

According to a statement, the state inquiry discovered that Juul advertised its e-cigarettes to underage minors via launch parties, product giveaways, and social media postings featuring young models.

In a statement to the media, Tong said that via the settlement, "we have obtained hundreds of millions of dollars to assist decrease nicotine use and forced Juul to accept a series of harsh injunctive restrictions to prohibit adolescent marketing and clamp down on underage sales."

The $438.5 million will be distributed over a six- to ten-year period. Tong said that Connecticut would contribute at least $16 million to measures to prevent and educate people about vaping. Prior legal disputes involving Juul were resolved in Arizona, Louisiana, North Carolina, and Washington. Payments under the $438.5 million settlement will be made over a six- to ten-year period. Alabama, Arkansas, Connecticut, Delaware, Georgia, Hawaii, Idaho, Indiana, Kansas, Kentucky, Maryland,

Maine, Mississippi, North Dakota, Nebraska, New Hampshire, New Jersey, Nevada, Ohio, Oklahoma, Oregon, Puerto Rico, Rhode Island, South Carolina, South Dakota, Tennessee, Utah, Virginia, Vermont, Wisconsin, and Wyoming are among the states and territories that are party to the settlement.

Juul has already stopped several of its product advertisements.

The majority of the restrictions imposed by the settlement announced on Tuesday 6th September, 2022 won't have an impact on Juul's business activities, since the company stopped using parties, freebies, and other promotions years ago after facing criticism.

Following years of regulatory delays, the FDA study is a part of a broad effort by authorities to scrutinize the multibillion-dollar vaping sector. Several e-cigarettes for adult smokers seeking a less dangerous option have been approved by the government.

The business has changed how it markets its products to elderly smokers.

Juul used to appeal to youthful, urban users, but it has now started positioning its product as a substitute for tobacco for elderly smokers.

The business added in a statement, "We remain focused on our future as we accomplish our commitment to transition adult smokers away from cigarettes, the leading cause of avoidable death, while combatting underage usage.

As part of the settlement, Juul has agreed to desist from a number of marketing techniques. They include refraining from employing cartoons, paying influencers on social media, portraying persons under 35, posting advertisements on billboards and in public transit, and refraining from placing advertisements in any outlets unless 85% of their audience is made up of adults.

The agreement also specifies limitations on both online and offline sales as well as placement restrictions for Juul products in retail locations.

Juul originally offered tastes including mango, mint, and crème for its high-nicotine pods. Students who vape in restrooms and halls in between classes have made the items a blight at high schools in the United States.

However, new government survey data indicates that youthful interest in the corporation is waning. Nowadays, the majority of teenagers choose disposable e-cigarettes, some of which are still offered in sweet, fruity flavors.

As many children were compelled to study at home during the epidemic, the poll overall revealed a decline in the incidence of adolescent vaping of over 40%. Despite this, federal authorities advised against interpreting the data since they were first gathered online rather than in classrooms.

www.ingramcontent.com/pod-product-compliance
Lightning Source LLC
LaVergne TN
LVHW052044160826
845678LV00015B/3110

* 9 7 9 8 3 5 1 6 6 4 4 7 7 *